FOOD FOOD FOOD

D1033319

OTHER BOOKS BY S. GROSS

How Gross

I Am Blind and My Dog Is Dead

An Elephant Is Soft and Mushy

More Gross

Why Are Your Papers in Order?

Dogs Dogs Dogs

Cats Cats Cats

Books Books Books

Golf Golf Golf

FOOD FOOD FOOD

a feast of great food cartoons

edited by S. Gross

PERENNIAL LIBRARY

HARPER & ROW, PUBLISHERS, New York
Grand Rapids, Philadelphia, St. Louis, San Francisco
London, Singapore, Sydney, Tokyo

Grateful acknowledgment is made to *The New Yorker* for permission to reprint cartoons which, as indicated throughout this book, originally appeared in that magazine.

A hardcover edition of this book was published in 1987 by Harper & Row, Publishers, under the title *All You Can Eat*.

FOOD FOOD FOOD. Copyright © 1987 by Sam Gross. All rights reserved. Printed in the United States of America. No part of this book may be used or reproduced in any manner whatsoever without written permission except in the case of brief quotations embodied in critical articles and reviews. For information address Harper & Row, Publishers, Inc., 10 East 53rd Street, New York, N.Y. 10022.

First PERENNIAL LIBRARY edition published 1989.

LIBRARY OF CONGRESS CATALOG CARD NUMBER 87-45054
ISBN 0-06-091638-9

---

89 90 91 92 93 HOR 10 9 8 7 6 5 4 3 2 1

"Let's just go in and see what happens."

GEORGE BOOTH

© 1986 The New Yorker Magazine, Inc.

“It’s going to be great!
All natural ingredients.”

CHARLES ADDAMS

© 1981 The New Yorker Magazine, Inc.

AARON BACALL

"How nouvelle is your cuisine?"

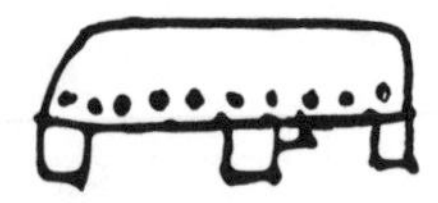

LOU MYERS

L. TREPEL

BORIS DRUCKER

"I like New York because there's a world-famous restaurant opening every day."

SIDNEY HARRIS

"This looks good. The first ingredient is whole wheat flour."

SAM GROSS

"Welcome to 'Bagel World.'"

LIZA DONNELLY

"They ran out of hog dogs, so I got you a tofu burger with sprouts."

LEE LORENZ

© 1978 The New Yorker Magazine, Inc.

"There you are . . . eggs Benedict"

PETER PORGES

“Five blocks of quiche places and not one shoe repair.”

DAVID PASCAL

MARTY MURPHY

"I could never hold a job as a chef 'cause
I burned the food and put too much spice in it.
Then—voila—along comes the Cajun craze."

SIDNEY HARRIS

". . . recalling Sun Glo orange juice, Corn-X
cereal and Lift coffee . . ."

1.75 PORK FRIED RICE 2.00
2.50 BEEF FRIED RICE 2.50
2.75 EGG ROLL .90
UPON REQUEST, WE WILL PRETEND NOT TO USE MSG.
L. TREPEL

L. TREPEL

“Explain to me the giant cookie phenomenon.”

"I never realized you knew how to use chopsticks!"

ELDON DEDINI

MARTY MURPHY

"Sorry . . . sir . . . rules . . . are . . . rules. . . . No . . . tie . . . no . . . service."

CATHERINE O'NEILL

"Angst. Weltschmerz. And now, my God, Wiener schnitzel!"

DICK OLDDEN

ED AND HIS CONSCIENCE GO TO LUNCH

EDWARD KOREN

© 1985 The New Yorker Magazine, Inc.

"Kate, this is the wonderful man I told you about who has such a strong hand with garlic and fresh thyme."

This is "Cuisine-o-Writer": the world's first word processor and food processor!
27"
SALE
SIPRESS
DAVID SIPRESS

"This is where Edgar goes for his power luncheons."

"Hi! I'm Marv and this is my partner, Ol' Blue. We'll be eating your leftovers tonight."

WARREN MILLER

CHARLES SAUERS
© 1984 The New Yorker Magazine, Inc.

"Everything that was bad for you is now good for you."

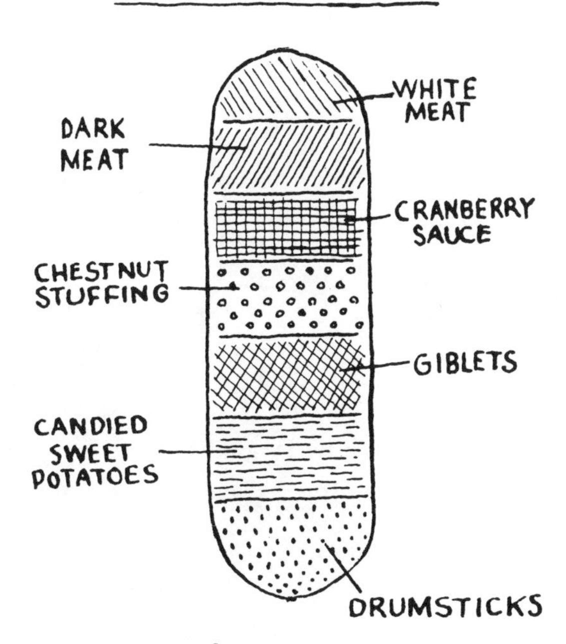

STUART LEEDS
© 1984 The New Yorker Magazine, Inc.

BRIAN SAVAGE

Where Are They Now?

R. Chast

ROZ CHAST

EDWARD FRASCINO

ED FISHER

© 1984 The New Yorker Magazine, Inc.

"This is my favorite spaghetti joint."

BUD GRACE

"We've got to stop taking our vitamins before dinner. I'm full."

BILL WOODMAN

INTRODUCING
THE PROVOLONE RANGER

MICHAEL CRAWFORD

JACK ZIEGLER

"Is there any ketchup in the house?"

© 1984 The New Yorker Magazine, Inc.

"For a more complete answer to that question, let us turn now to the *Book of Tofu.*"

CATHERINE O'NEILL

"It's pasta primavera!"

BUD GRACE

SAM GROSS

M.K. BROWN

© 1980 The New Yorker Magazine, Inc.

MICHAEL MASLIN

"He claims I summoned him with my special blend of herbs and spices."

"I can't eat anymore, Fred,
and I can't run anymore."

ELDON DEDINI

MORT GERBERG

No, no, I ordered pot au feu, not pot le fou!"

SAM GROSS

KASHA HUT
PLATE OF KASHA, HEAPED WITH FRESH KASHA, AND TOPPED WITH KASHA $4.99
MORSELS OF TENDER KASHA SWIMMING IN A KASHA SAUCE $4.99
KASHA WITH MELTED KASHA ON A BUN $2.99
DEEP-FRIED KASHA $2.99
KASHA DU JOUR $3.99
BABY KASHA SERVED WITH YOUR CHOICE OF KASHA OR KASHA $3.99
SIZZLING 16 oz. OF KASHA WITH SIDE OF KASHA $5.99
KASHA STUFFED WITH KASHA $2.99
R. Chast

ROZ CHAST

AL ROSS

"Congratulations, you are now an educated wine drinker. Congratulations, you are now an educated wine drinker. Congratulations . . ."

ELDON DEDINI

"Remember, Marco, al dente on the noodles."

"Enzo writes that he's getting eighteen thousand lire for a plate of tagliatelle al formaggio on the lower East Side—and that's for *lunch!*"

DONALD REILLY

© 1986 The New Yorker Magazine, Inc.

J.B. HANDELSMAN

© 1985 The New Yorker Magazine, Inc.

"That may be Craig Claiborne. I asked him to come over with his wok."

HENRY MARTIN

© 1974 The New Yorker Magazine, Inc.

WARREN MILLER

© 1983 The New Yorker Magazine, Inc.

it's a new scratch and sniff book.
Just scratch and sniff.

that's it! Now sniff.

Sniff!
sniff!

(continued) →

BILL WOODMAN

MICK STEVENS

© 1983 The New Yorker Magazine, Inc.

DAVID SIPRESS

"I'm sorry, sir, but our outdoor tables are reserved for people who look French."

CHARLES ADDAMS

© 1981 The New Yorker Magazine, Inc.

SIDNEY HARRIS

"Nutrition is very big these days. If anyone asks, tell them that nutrition is your prime concern."

AARON BACALL

“Don’t be alarmed. It’s our first time in the non-smoking section.”

BERNARD SCHOENBAUM

SAM GROSS

JACK ZIEGLER

"What I want to know is when the hell 'petite' became synonymous with 'nouvelle.'"

OLIVER CHRISTIANSON (REVILO)

"Eat lots of fibre, drink plenty of fluids and be merry."

“You ate it? That yogurt was for my hair.”

EDWARD FRASCINO

“This next piece is dedicated to you carrots over there.”

BILL WOODMAN

ELDON DEDINI

"The one on the left is her personal nutritionist.

LEE LORENZ

© 1985 The New Yorker Magazine, Inc.

WARREN MILLER

"Thanks."

"Great stuff!"

LEO CULLUM

© 1985 The New Yorker Magazine, Inc.

"I've got the Los Angeles office on the line.
Does anyone need avocados?"

THOMAS WUTHRICH (SWISS)

ROBERT MANKOFF

"When it came to raisins, Mom's motto was "Use your imagination."

HENRY MARTIN

© 1982 The New Yorker Magazine, Inc.

JARED LEE

"Of course, I ate my vegetables . . .
I'm a vegetarian!"

BILL WOODMAN

"Tell ya what, pal . . . let's just pretend I never heard you order those two wine coolers."

MARTY MURPHY

MASLIN
MICHAEL MASLIN

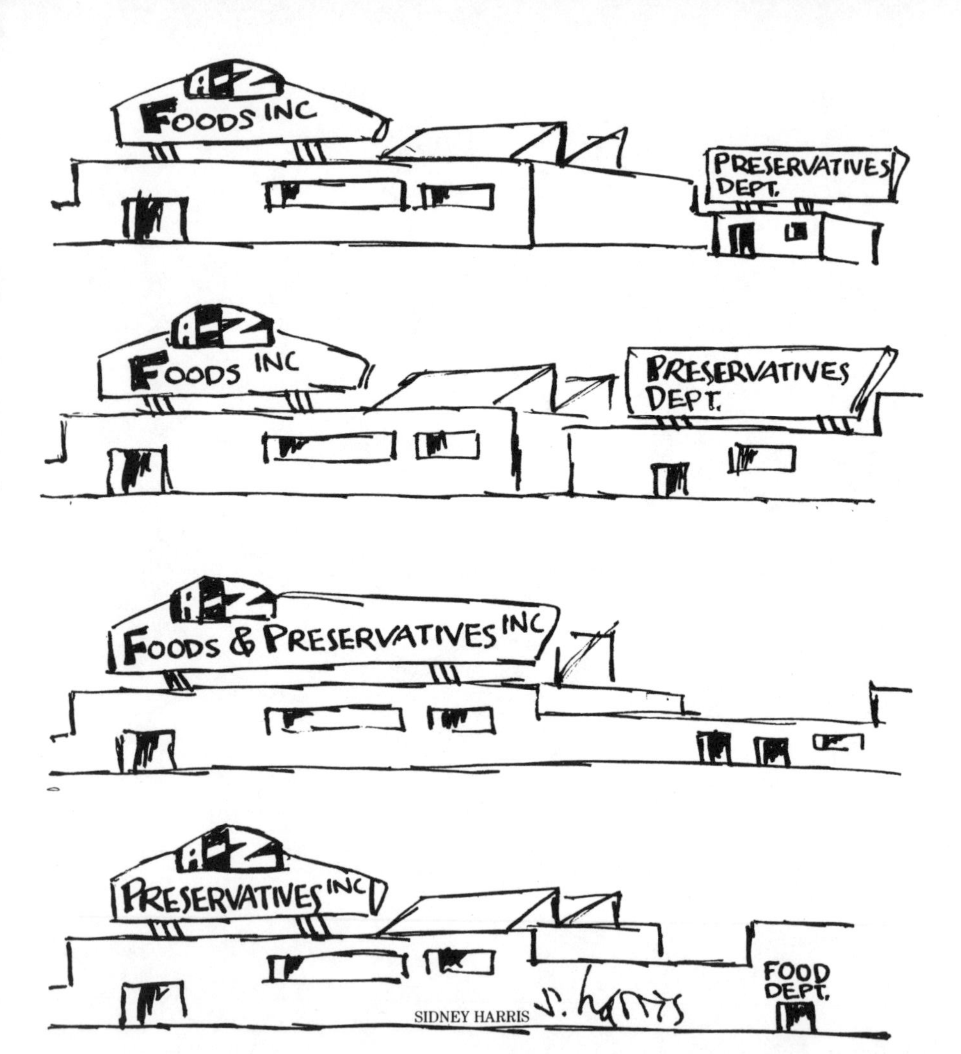

SIDNEY HARRIS

ELDON DEDINI

"I say it's designer food and to hell with it!"

SAM GROSS

"Your car will be ready in about an hour. Would you care to try our salad bar?"

CHICKENS of the 'Eighties

1 Minute Wonders ~
These hens cook up so fast, they'll take your breath away.

New England Neverspoils ~
You can keep these pullets around for months - even years - at room temperature. They'll never go bad

R. Chast

ROZ CHAST

NURIT KARLIN

HENRY MARTIN

“. . . and eight tubs of vanilla. Vanilla still seems to be the favorite.”

TONY ROSA

SIDNEY HARRIS

"In nouvelle cuisine, we never explain and we never apologize."

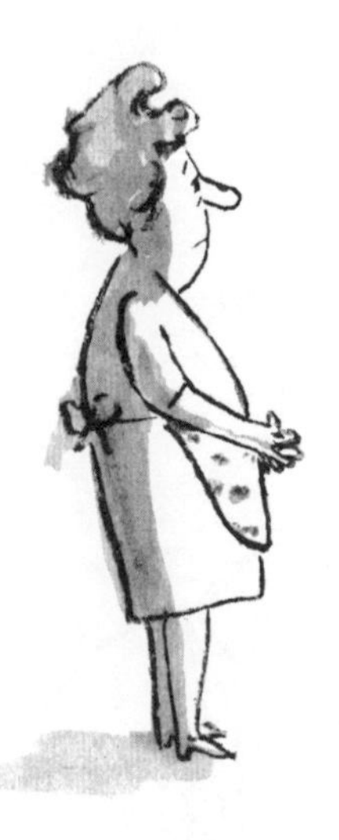

JAMES MULLIGAN

© 1984 The New Yorker Magazine, Inc.

"The zucchini's in!"

ORLANDO BUSINO

"Oh, no! Not junk food!"

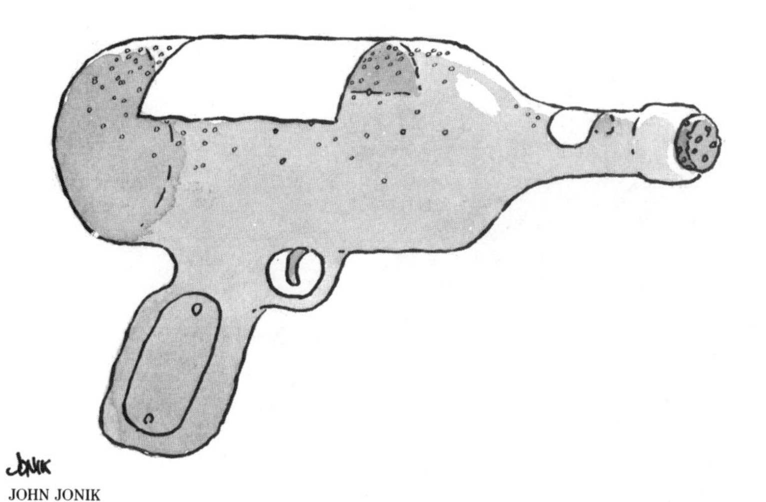

JOHN JONIK

EVOLUTION

DINOSAUR COFFEE

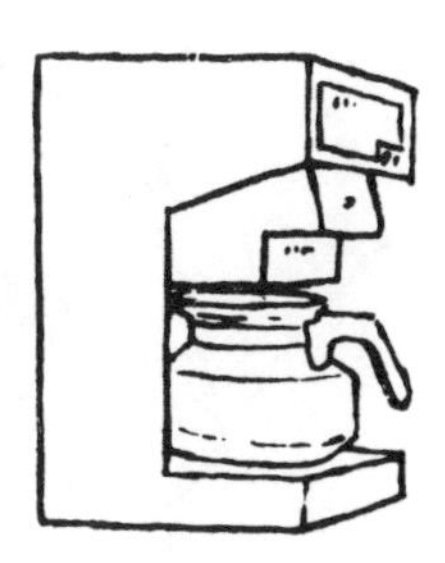

MR. COFFEE

STUART LEEDS

© 1983 The New Yorker Magazine, Inc.

"Here's your meatloaf, sir.
In case of emergency, it can be used as a flotation device."

WILLIAM HOEST

"I'm at a secret training camp somewhere in the foothills of Connecticut. Behind me—food and soft drink specialists, marching off to join the hamburger war."

"I swear by Paul Newman's spaghetti sauce.
Now, if only Robert Redford made a pasta."

SUSHI
ART'S BAIT SHOP
すし
OPEN
TACKLE
CHARTERS
SQUID
TIDE
OLDDEN

DICK OLDDEN

CLEM SCALSITTI

MICHAEL CRAWFORD

WARREN MILLER

"These are roasted, oil and salt; these are roasted, oil, no salt; these are dry roasted with salt; these are dry roasted without; these are sun-dried with salt; next are sun-dried without; and these are fresh and raw with nothing."

BRIAN SAVAGE

"Mrs. Ritterhouse had a dream last night. She dreamed about firm, fresh cucumbers, their skins uncoated with shelf-life-extending goop; tender zucchini and sweet corn; red, ripe, juicy tomatoes; big bunches of piquant basil; sprigs of herbs such as tarragon and sage. It's the same dream she had last year in February."

GEORGE BOOTH

© 1982 The New Yorker Magazine, Inc.

JACK ZIEGLER

LEE LORENZ

© 1986 The New Yorker Magazine, Inc.

"Is that with or without goat cheese?"

"There's No Chocolate in Hell

OLIVER CHRISTIANSON (REVILO)

EDWARD FRASCINO

"Hey, guys, I've put a twelve course dinner on the head of a pin."

THE END OF AN ERA: MAY 10, 1987:

Bean Sprouts Begin to Taste Weird

ROZ CHAST

"Ed, I thought you cancelled Fruit-of-the-Month."

"Wow! Chocolate truffles. Can I have one?"

HENRY MARTIN

© 1986 The New Yorker Magazine, Inc.

"He was a man of simple tastes—
baked macaroni, steamed cabbage, wax beans,
boiled onions, and corn fritters."

MICK STEVENS

J. B. HANDELSMAN

"Miss, this seems to be blackened redfish. We would have preferred reddened blackfish."

STUART LEEDS

CHARLES SAUERS

"I want the secret of your barbecue sauce."

BILL WOODMAN

TIM HAGGERTY